101 American English Proverbs

Understanding Language and Culture
Through Commonly Used Sayings

D1235745

American English Proverbs

Harry Collis

Illustrated by Mario Risso

New York Chicago San Francisco Lisbon London Madrid Mexico City
Milan New Delhi San Juan Seoul Singapore Sydney Toronto

1 2 3 4 5 6 7 8 9 10 11 12 13 14 15 16 17 18 19 20 21   FGR/FGR   0 9

ISBN 978-0-07-161588-4 (book and MP3 disk set)
MHID   0-07-161588-1 (book and MP3 disk set)

ISBN 978-0-07-161550-1 (book for set)
MHID   0-07-161550-4 (book for set)

Library of Congress Control Number: 2008935417

MP3 Files

The disk contains MP3 audio recordings that accompany the book.
    To download: Double-click on MY COMPUTER, find and open your CD-ROM disk drive and double-click on the 101 American English Proverbs Idioms icon.
    The MP3 files can be played on your computer and loaded onto your MP3 player. For optimum use on the iPod:

1. Open iTunes on your computer.
2. Drag folder "Copy to iTunes Music Library" into the Music Library in the iTunes menu.
3. Sync your iPod with iTunes and eject iPod.
4. Locate recordings on your iPod by following this path:
    Main menu: Music
    Music menu: Artists
    Artist menu: 101 American English Proverbs

Call 1-800-722-4726 if the MP3 disk is missing from this book.
For technical support go to
http://www.mhprofessional.com/support/technical/contact.php

This book is printed on acid-free paper.

Contents

invention □ No pain, no gain □ Nothing ventured, nothing gained □ The pen is mightier than the sword □ Practice makes perfect □ Rome wasn't built in a day □ The squeaking wheel gets the oil □ You're never too old to learn

Foreword

Proverbs, by stating basic principles of folk wisdom and conduct, have become an essential and enduring part of daily speech in all societies. Very often the precepts of one culture are precepts of another, for they are an outgrowth of common experiences.

Each language has its own proverbs. The phrasing is unique and contributes to the color of the language. But whatever the phraseological turns, many proverbs convey similar meanings in different forms. For example, the Spanish proverb *Dime con quien andas y te dire quien eres* ("Tell me with whom you associate, and I'll tell you who you are") finds an equivalent in the English proverb *A man is known by the company he keeps*. The French *Jamais deux sans trois* ("Never two without three") corresponds to the English *It never rains but it pours*.

Proverbs are relatively easy for nonnative speakers to learn and use. Once the concept of the proverb is understood, students can often relate it to similar concepts, in their own languages—whereas correct, natural usage of idioms requires more practice and a better "feel" for the language.

101 American English Proverbs is designed to help students of English understand and use proverbs that relate to everyday situations. The proverbs in this book are grouped in nine thematic sections, in order to facilitate student understanding and acquisition of proverbs for use in particular contexts. Within each section the proverbs are listed alphabetically.

The proverbs included in **101 American English Proverbs** are among those that are most familiar to and most frequently used by native speakers of English. Each proverb is presented in its most common form together with a standard English definition. It must be noted that many of the proverbs have variant forms as well as more than one possible meaning. Students are unlikely to be troubled by this flexibility if they reflect on its presence in the proverbs of their native languages. The wordings and definitions selected for this book are intended to help students achieve a basic understanding of each proverb.

A cartoon and a short paragraph or dialogue are provided to help illustrate the meaning and usage of each proverb. The paragraphs and dialogues serve two purposes: to give an understanding of the proverb in a normal everyday setting and to enhance the student's awareness of natural American speech. To this end they include many contemporary expressions. These expressions should not deter from the basic comprehension of the proverb. The illustrations add an element of humor while helping to convey the meaning of each proverb.

An index is included to facilitate recall and location of the proverbs. The standard English definitions for the proverbs are also listed in the index.

101 American English Proverbs is an excellent tool for teaching an aspect of English that is such an integral part of the language. This book also serves as a springboard for conversation about some of the similarities and differences between various languages and cultures. Both nonnative and native speakers of English will benefit from and enjoy the wealth of linguistic and cultural information to be found in this selection of 101 American English proverbs.

Section One

All Together Now

Birds of a Feather Flock Together

(people of the same type seem to gather together)

I haven't seen Mark lately. Do you know where he's been?

As far as I know, he's still hanging around with those rock musicians. He's been attending their rehearsals, hoping to pick up a few pointers.

Birds of a feather flock together. I know he wants to start his own group, so I guess I shouldn't be surprised that he hasn't had much time for his buddies. Still, I'd like to hear from him just to see how it's going.

People with the same interests do tend to associate with each other. But I agree with you; that's no excuse for not keeping in touch with old friends.

1

In Unity There Is Strength

(a group of people with the same goals can accomplish more than individuals can)

If we want better working conditions, we've got to get together and make up a list of grievances to present to the administration.

But what makes you think they'll listen to us?

In unity there is strength! We won't get anywhere by complaining individually. **We can accomplish more as a group than we can by ourselves.**

That makes sense. Let's call a meeting of all the employees of the shop. We can pin down our demands and present a united front. Maybe we'll get someplace this time.

It Takes Two to Tango

(when two people work as a team, they are both responsible for the team's successes and failures)

Look how crooked the linoleum is along the edges of the wall. It looks just awful!

I never said I was an expert in laying linoleum. Besides, **it takes two to tango.**

Just what do you mean by that?

Well, you're the one who gave me the measurements. If the job turned out badly **it was just as much your fault as it was mine.**

Maybe so, but if you'll remember, I wanted to hire a professional to do the job. You were the one who thought we should save money by doing it ourselves.

I guess we both learned a lesson. Next time we'll know better.

A Man Is Known by the Company He Keeps

(a person is believed to be like the people with whom he or she spends time)

Come here, Glenn. As your friend, I've got to tell you that people are starting to wonder why you're hanging around with all those anti-government demonstrators.

Look. We've been friends ever since our college days. I'm not doing anything wrong.

Maybe not, but since you work for a government agency, you've got to be more careful about who you associate with. **A man is known by the company he keeps.**

Guilty by association. Is that it?

Unfortunately, yes. **People often believe that a person is like his friends.**

Boy, what a hassle! Now what do I do?

If I were you, I'd cool it with those pals of yours for a while.

4

Misery Loves Company

(unhappy people often get satisfaction from having others share their misery)

Hey Misha, what's wrong?

Oh, I just had a run-in with my math teacher over the grading of my last exam. Although I got a wrong answer on one of the problems, I did use a correct equation and he refused to give me even partial credit.

Don't feel so blue. You're not alone. I'm kind of in the same boat myself, only with my history teacher. I got a really low grade because she didn't like my essay.

Although **misery loves company**, I don't feel any better knowing that you're in the same predicament.

At least I tried. I thought **you might get some comfort from knowing that someone else shared your misery.**

There's No Place like Home

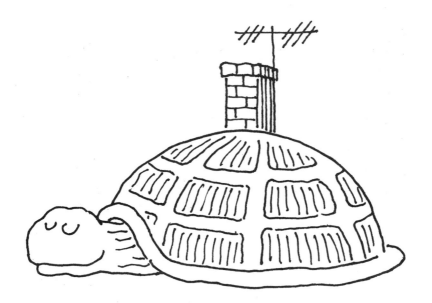

(a person is happiest with his or her family and friends)

Pamela was fond of traveling, and she always enjoyed seeing exotic lands and peoples. However, after experiencing the thrill of cultures other than her own for a while, she would eventually begin to yearn for her native land and to think that **there's no place like home**. The museums, the architecture, the food, the music, and the culture of faraway places fascinated Pamela, but she never forgot that **the place where she felt the happiest and most comfortable was in her own home with her family and friends.**

Too Many Cooks Spoil the Broth

(too many people trying to take care of something can ruin it)

What are you doing, Benito?

I'm trying to fix the copy machine. I'll have it going again soon if everybody stops making suggestions.

Well, you can't blame the other employees for being impatient to run off their materials. They just want to help you.

Yeah, **but too many cooks spoil the broth**. They really don't know what they're doing, and if I listened to their advice this would never get fixed. I'm the guy with the experience, and **I don't want to have the machine ruined by too many people trying to fix it.** Just let me be, and I'll handle it on my own.

Two Heads Are Better Than One

(two people working together can solve a problem quicker and better than a person working alone)

Hey, Jonathan. Come over here a minute.

What's happening?

I'd like to pick your brain for this composition I have to hand in tomorrow. I've got a problem with the introduction, and I figure that **two heads are better than one**. I need some input on the wording.

To be honest with you, I'm not that good with words, but I'm willing to help out if I can.

Thanks, buddy. My brain is all dried up. I'm sure **the two of us working together will be able to solve this problem faster than I could do it alone.**

Well, I'll give it my best shot. Let me look at what you've already written and we'll take it from there.

Two's Company,
but Three's a Crowd

(couples often enjoy their privacy and dislike having a third person around)

How did your date with Nari go the other night?

Everything started out OK, but just as we started to talk seriously about our plans for the future, Bob came barging in and interrupted our conversation.

What a pain! **Two's company, but three's a crowd.**

You said it! I wanted to take him aside and tell him that Nari and I were having a serious conversation and that **his presence was an intrusion on our privacy,** but when I remembered how few friends he has since he's new in town, I decided not to say anything.

Did you ever get back to your conversation?

Yeah. We were able to pick it up again after Bob left.

Section Two

Try This

An Apple a Day Keeps the Doctor Away

(eating an apple every day helps a person to stay healthy)

Boy, do I ever feel lousy! I don't have any energy lately. Have you been eating a lot of junk food?

Now that you mention it, I have, but I don't think that alone could account for my fatigue. It's got to be something else. I'm going to see my doctor tomorrow and have her check me out.

Fine—but in the future, that might not be necessary if you watch what you eat. Don't you know that **an apple a day keeps the doctor away?**

Sure. I've heard that proverb before, but I've never taken it seriously. I can't believe that **just by eating one apple a day I'll stay healthy and strong and won't ever need to see a doctor.**

Try it! You might like it. What do you have to lose?

Do As I Say, Not As I Do

(follow my advice, but don't follow my example)

For heaven's sake, Dave. You smell like a chimney. How many times do I have to tell you that smoking is going to eat out your lungs and take years off your life?

You can talk all you want—but look at you!

Never mind me. **Do as I say, not as I do**.

But you've been smoking ever since you were a teenager.

Just because I made a mistake doesn't mean you have to repeat it. I'm telling you to **follow my advice, not my example**.

OK. You win. I'll try. But why don't we *both* try to stop? Maybe we can help each other out.

You're on. I'll give it a whirl.

If You Can't Beat Them, Join Them

**(if you can't defeat your opponents,
join forces with them)**

Mrs. Kowalski had never been much of a sports fan—
unlike her husband and two children. On weekends the
others would take in either a baseball or a football game,
while she stayed home alone. After a while the situation
became a source of great annoyance to her. One weekend,
to the utter amazement of her husband and children, she
announced that she wanted to attend the football game
with them. She thought, **If you can't beat them, join
them.** Mrs. Kowalski realized that **since she could not talk
her family out of attending the games, she might as well
join them in one of their favorite pastimes**. By joining her
family on the weekends she would alleviate her
loneliness, and in time she might even come to like sports
as much as her husband and children did.

If You Can't Stand the Heat, Get Out of the Kitchen

(if you can't tolerate the pressures of a particular situation, remove yourself from that situation)

When Chris got a position as a legal secretary with one of the most prestigious law firms in the city, he was elated. However, it was not long before he became snowed under with work. As the pressures of the job increased, he began to complain about the long hours and the excessive amount of work. One day, after a fellow employee heard him complain once again about the stack of paperwork on his desk, she quite bluntly told him: **If you can't stand the heat, get out of the kitchen.** Actually, Chris had been thinking about quitting. After only three months on the job, it became apparent to him that **since he could not handle the pressures of the job, he should leave the firm** and seek employment elsewhere. The only reason he had been hanging on was because good jobs were so hard to come by.

Leave Well Enough Alone

(don't try to improve something that is already satisfactory)

Greetings, Vicki. What have you been up to lately?

Oh, I've been busy working on my sculpture for the spring art exhibition. I'm just not satisfied with the symmetry between the head and the torso.

I'm no connoisseur, but when I saw your sculpture last week I was very impressed. Really, Vicki. Don't change a thing! **Leave well enough alone!** If you keep trying to improve your sculpture, you might end up ruining it.

Do you really think so?

Absolutely. **There's no reason for you to change something that is already satisfactory**.

Maybe you're right. I'll sleep on it and see how I feel about the whole thing tomorrow.

Look before You Leap

(consider all aspects of a situation before you take any action)

You sure are concentrating! What's so interesting?

Oh. Hi, Ed. I didn't hear you come in. I'm thinking of investing in that shopping center going up near Tiburon Beach, so I was just reading about the proposed shops for the center.

If you want my opinion, I think **you should look before you leap**. That center is being built on a landfill. Aren't you wary of problems with settling, let alone an earthquake?

Have no fear! **I'm considering all aspects of the situation before I take any action.** But from what I've read so far, it sounds like a great investment.

Make Hay While the Sun Shines

(take advantage of an opportunity to do something)

Come on, Jed. Don't be such a wet blanket! Come with us to the state fair.

I'd like to, but I'm swamped with work. Maybe next time.

That's what you're always saying, and next time never comes. You're young. **Make hay while the sun shines.** Trips like this one don't come around every day.

I'm really tempted, but I've got to finish this paperwork.

Meanwhile, life is passing you right by. **You should take advantage of an opportunity to do something when it's available.** Doesn't the fact that Mary Ann will be coming along tempt you?

Mary Ann is going?

Absolutely.

Well, maybe just this once I could take a break from working. OK. Count me in!

Strike While the Iron Is Hot

(act at the best possible time)

If you intend to make an offer on that house you were thinking of buying, now is the time to do it.

But I can only offer considerably less than what the owner is asking. I don't know if she'll accept.

I recommend that you **strike while the iron is hot**. It's a buyer's market right now. It's a good time to make an offer, even if it is low.

Hmm. I do like the house. I guess I'll give it a try. As you said, **my chances for success are greater if I act at the best possible time.**

That's right. If you make an offer now, there's an excellent chance that it will be accepted.

The Way to a Man's Heart Is through His Stomach

(the way to gain a man's love is by preparing food that he enjoys)

Wow, Ludmilla! You look beautiful! What's the big occasion?

I've got a date with Yuri. I hope that tonight he'll come out and tell me how much he cares for me.

You've been going with Yuri for quite some time. If he still hasn't expressed his feelings, I think you ought to try another approach. Have you ever stopped to think that **the way to a man's heart is through his stomach**? You're a fantastic cook. Why not invite him to a nice home-cooked meal?

Why didn't I think of that before? Tonight I'll invite him to have dinner at my place next weekend.

There you go! **Prepare a meal that he enjoys, and he'll love you for sure!**

When in Rome Do As the Romans Do

(when traveling, follow the customs of the local people)

Jane and Ray had been homebodies most of their lives, but after their kids were grown and out of the nest, they decided to take a trip around the world. Of course, they were inexperienced travelers and they had trouble accepting the customs of the people in the countries they visited. To make them feel more comfortable during their travels, some members of the tour group recommended that **when in Rome do as the Romans do**. They suggested that Jane and Ray **should make an effort to follow the customs of the local inhabitants** and not expect to behave in a foreign country as they would at home. Once they began to follow this advice, Jane and Ray enjoyed their trip much more.

19

Section Three

Watch Out!

All That Glitters Is Not Gold

(some things are not as valuable as they appear to be)

Boy, Ahmed sure got taken the other day at the bazaar. What happened?

You know he collects old swords and sabers. Well, he came across a neat, shining scimitar in one of the booths. The guy assured him that it dated from the fifteenth century and that it would never rust. Ahmed was so excited with his find that he really didn't examine it very carefully before he took it home. That's when he discovered that the scimitar was coated to hide the rust and that it was a copy, not an original.

Just goes to prove that **all that glitters is not gold**.

That's for sure! Ahmed learned the hard way that **some things are not as valuable as they appear to be**.

Curiosity Killed the Cat

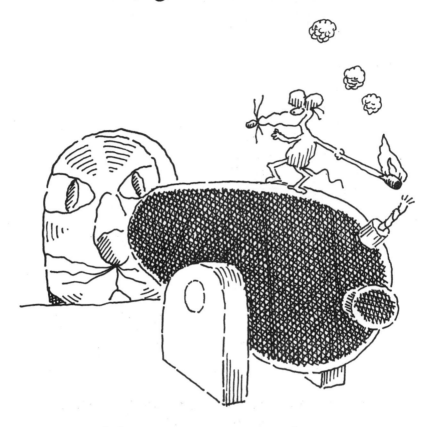

(it is dangerous to be curious)

Phil, you have no business trying to find out what will be on tomorrow's exam by shuffling through those papers on the teacher's desk. Just because she's out of the room doesn't give you the right to go poking in her personal papers. What do you think will happen to you if she walks in and catches you? Don't you realize that **curiosity killed the cat**?

If I don't pass this exam, I probably won't pass the course. I know **I could be severely punished for going into her personal papers**, but I'm desperate!

OK. But it's your funeral! Sooner or later your curiosity will do you in.

Don't Bite Off More Than You Can Chew

(don't assume more responsibility than you can handle; don't be overconfident)

Hold on there, Sam. Where are you running off to?

Oh, hi Lloyd. Can't stop to chat. I'm already late for work.

It seems like you're always busy lately. If it's not work, it's studies or something else. You don't have time for your friends anymore. When you took that full-time job I warned you: **Don't bite off more than you can chew**!

I think you were right. Now I see that **it was a mistake to take on too much responsibility all at once.** My grades in school are already starting to go down.

There you are! Why don't you cut down on your hours at work and maybe drop a course or two, at least for this semester?

Maybe I'll do that. At this rate my health is liable to suffer, too.

Don't Bite the Hand That Feeds You

(don't hurt someone who takes care of you)

Julie, I simply can't understand you! I've worked my fingers to the bone and I've saved and scrimped to pay for your college education, and here you go running off to get married without finishing school. Hasn't anyone ever told you, **"Don't bite the hand that feeds you"**? You must know how disappointed I am!

I'm sorry, Dad. **I don't mean to hurt you after all you've done for me**, and I have every intention of going back to school after Al and I get settled. He's got a great job overseas, and he wants me to go with him as his wife.

Still, I find it difficult to approve of your decision to quit school now, when you're about to get your degree. Don't be hasty. Why don't you give this a little bit more thought?

Don't Count Your Chickens
Before They're Hatched

**(don't plan on the successful results of
something until those results actually occur)**

Hi, Lydia. How are you doing with your book about
the Indian tribes of the Amazon?

I haven't found a publisher yet, but I know it will be a
big success. I'm going to use the money from my advance
royalties as a down payment on that condo I've been
looking at.

Don't count your chickens before they're hatched.
What if you can't find a publisher?

I guess you're right. **I really should not count on
getting any money until the book is actually accepted for
publication**.

And even then the publishers may not advance you
enough for a down payment on that condo. But don't
despair. It's quite possible that someone out there will
want to publish your book. I wish you all the best.

Don't Cry over Spilt Milk

**(don't grieve about having done something that
cannot be undone)**

Lois, why are you so upset?

Oh, Andy, I'm glad you're back. I don't know what to
do. I was cleaning the house and I knocked over the
crystal vase we received as a wedding gift from your
folks. It fell to the floor and shattered.

Come on, now. **Don't cry over spilt milk**.

But I can't help being upset. That vase had a lot of
sentimental value for both of us.

Relax. It can be replaced. Mom and Dad will
understand. **It won't do any good to keep crying about
something that can't be undone.** Let's go out to dinner.
I'm sure you'll feel better once you get away from the
house.

You're probably right. Thanks, honey.

Don't Judge a Book by Its Cover

(don't form an opinion about something based on appearance alone)

Have you seen the new guy they hired as coach of Commodore High's football team? He's so short and puny. He hardly looks like a football coach to me.

Listen, pal. **Don't judge a book by its cover.** From what I hear, that guy is one of the best. His size has nothing to do with his ability to produce a winning team.

How do you know that?

I was talking with one of the players on the team. He said that the new coach is a genius at strategies on the football field, and he puts the team through some of the roughest training they've ever had.

That surprises me. I guess **I really shouldn't base my opinion about him on the way he looks**.

Don't Judge a Man until You've Walked in His Boots

(don't criticize a person until you've tried to do the things he or she does)

Hi, Josh. Did you watch the gymnastic competitions on TV last night?

I sure did. Those guys were phenomenal on the bars and rings!

All except the short, blond guy. His performance was really weak. I don't see why he even bothered to compete.

Look. **Don't judge a man until you've walked in his boots.** You've probably never tried to do the things he was doing. I'll bet you couldn't even hold your balance on those rings.

OK. Maybe **I shouldn't go around criticizing another person's performance until I've tried it myself,** but it seemed to me that the other athletes were vastly superior.

Oh, come on now. He wasn't that bad. His maneuvers were a lot more difficult than those of his competitors.

Don't Look a Gift Horse in the Mouth

(don't complain about something that is given to you)

How are you enjoying your car, Mike?

It's not bad. It doesn't look like much, but at least it's transportation.

Didn't your dad just give it to you outright?

Sure, but it was his old one. What I really wanted was that sleek sports car I was looking at the other day.

For gosh sakes, Mike. **Don't look a gift horse in the mouth.** If I were you, I wouldn't complain. Look at me. I'm still getting around on my bike.

I guess you're right. **I shouldn't find fault with something I got for nothing.**

Exactly! You'll have the car you want some day. Just be patient. All you have to do is get yourself a job and save money.

Don't Put All Your Eggs in One Basket

(don't risk losing everything at once)

Congratulations, Jill. I hear that you came into quite an inheritance.

Yes, I did. My grandmother left me the bulk of her estate when she passed away. Now I'll have to start thinking of ways to invest it if I want to see it grow.

True. And remember: **don't put all your eggs in one basket**.

Never fear. **I won't risk losing my money by investing all of it in a single place.** I plan to spread out my inheritance in real estate, government bonds, and other low-risk investments.

Now you're talking! If you're interested, I have the name of a good financial counselor. I'm certain that she could help you.

Thanks. As soon as I'm ready, I'll look her up.

Don't Put Off for Tomorrow What You Can Do Today

(don't unnecessarily postpone doing something)

My gosh, Kathy. Why are you so late for work?

Problems with my car again. The motor kept overheating. I just barely made it here.

Your car has been acting up for some time now. Didn't you say you were going to have it serviced last week?

Yes, I did. But I just didn't get to it.

When will you ever learn? **Don't put off for tomorrow what you can do today**!

You're right. I've got to realize that **I should not delay in taking care of something that needs to be done**. If I leave it until another time, I'll forget about it and it'll never get done.

Don't Put the Cart before the Horse

(don't do things in the wrong order)

Come on, Stanley. Let's go over to the stereo shop. I'd like to buy a big screen TV set and a pair of those tower speakers while they're on sale.

Whoa, there. **Don't put the cart before the horse!** Didn't you tell me that you were going to be cramped for space in your new apartment?

Yes, I did.

Then **don't go out and buy something that may not fit before you have all your other furniture in place**. What's more important—buying a new TV and speakers or moving in all the belongings you have already?

I guess you're right. I'd better wait until I see how much space I have.

A Miss Is As Good As a Mile

(losing by a narrow margin is no different than losing by a wide margin)

Why so glum, chum?

I was just one number away from winning big on the state lottery.

At least you won something, didn't you?

Something is right. About fifty bucks. But just think, one more number and I could have won thousands!

Too bad. But **a miss is as good as a mile**.

I understand that **losing by a narrow margin is no different than losing by a wide margin**. Still, it hurts to know that I was so close.

Yeah. Losing out by just one number is hard to take. But brighten up. Maybe you'll have better luck next time.

The Road to Hell Is Paved with Good Intentions

(good intentions don't always lead to good actions)

Erik, when are you going to repair the roof? You've been talking about it for a month now.

Andrea, I wish you wouldn't keep nagging me. I have every intention of getting to it this weekend.

Sure. **The road to hell is paved with good intentions.** How long are you going to keep putting it off?

Well, something always comes up. I should be able to start it on Saturday morning.

Let's see what happens. I won't say another word about it if you really mean what you say. I just get annoyed when **your good intentions don't lead to good actions**.

Have faith! I'll do it this weekend for sure.

Where There's Smoke, There's Fire

(when there is evidence of a problem, there probably is a problem)

When the night watchman started on his routine patrol of the premises, he noticed that the door to one of the buildings was ajar. Since the building was located in a security area, he immediately jumped to the conclusion that **where there's smoke, there's fire**. The doors of all the buildings were supposed to be tightly secured after working hours, and the night watchman had been trained to think that **if there's evidence of a problem, there probably is a problem.**

Section Four

Getting Ahead

The First Step Is Always the Hardest

(the most difficult part of accomplishing something is getting started)

Well, Adam. Did you enjoy the concert?

Yes, I did. It was quite inspiring. I sure wish I could play the violin like the concert artist who performed this evening.

There's no reason why you can't. **The first step is always the hardest.** You're still young. All you have to do is make up your mind to work at it.

Do you really think I'll ever be able to play like her?

It's hard to say at this point. But if you have enough talent and if you work hard enough, you can realize your wish. **The hardest part of learning to play like that is to start taking lessons and to learn to read music.** If you're serious about starting, I have the name of an excellent music teacher.

Wonderful. I'll give her a call the first thing tomorrow.

Forewarned Is Forearmed

(being warned about something before it happens allows a person to prepare for it)

When it became known that a hurricane was due to hit the coast within twenty-four hours, the local authorities **alerted the inhabitants and outlined a series of precautionary measures for coping with the storm**. Their goal was to avoid having people harmed by the devastating force of the winds and rain. The authorities rightly believed that **forewarned is forearmed**.

He Who Hesitates Is Lost

(a person who doesn't act decisively is unlikely to succeed)

If you want to buy that new car you've been looking at, you'd better hurry up.

Why?

Don't you read the papers? Next month the state sales tax is going up a whole cent. That will add up to a lot of money on a car! **He who hesitates is lost.**

I've been holding off because the dealer told me there would soon be a factory-authorized rebate on the car I want. But I see your point. **If I delay in purchasing the car, I may never get another chance to buy it at the current price.** Maybe I'd better not wait for the factory rebate—especially if it comes through after the new taxes go into effect.

Wise decision. Get hopping!

If at First You Don't Succeed, Try, Try Again

(persevere until you reach your goal)

You know, if anybody deserves a medal for valiant effort and accomplishment, it's Joanna. I remember when she went back to running the hurdles after her accident. In spite of the pain she suffered from her injuries, she kept on exercising until she was able to run again.

I agree. Joanna is a living example of the proverb: **If at first you don't succeed, try, try again**.

That's true. She would not allow herself to accept defeat. During the course of her recovery, she often stumbled and fell and many people thought she would never be able to run again. But Joanna fooled them all! **She kept working until she achieved her goal.** What a gal!

Necessity Is the Mother of Invention

(most inventions are created to solve a problem)

It's so good to see you, Fred. I was really distressed to hear that you lost your home in the recent hurricane. Is everything OK now?

We're alive and kicking, but for a while there it was touch and go. That hurricane hit us full blast.

Wow! How did you manage to survive?

Well, you know that **necessity is the mother of invention**. We built a makeshift shelter from the ruins until help arrived.

That must have taken some doing.

It sure did! **Being in such a difficult situation forced us to be creative.**

What an experience!

You said it! We were lucky to come out of it alive.

No Pain, No Gain

(nothing can be accomplished without effort)

Is Chiqui off practicing again?

Yes, that's all she does. She's up at four in the morning, and by five she's already at the ice rink. She puts in two full hours of practice before going to school. Then after school, she practices for another three hours with her partner.

That's a crushing routine. How does she do it?

No pain, no gain. She wants to be a champion ice skater, so she's working hard to perfect her technique and skills.

At this rate she'll make it by the time she's out of high school.

Maybe even sooner. She is one determined young lady. She knows that **without great effort and discipline she'll never achieve her goal.**

Nothing Ventured, Nothing Gained

(you can't achieve anything if you don't try)

For years Tanya dreamed of participating in the
ice-skating competitions in the Olympics. When tryouts
for the team were announced, Tanya doubted that she
could qualify, but she thought: **nothing ventured, nothing
gained**. After all, she knew that **if she didn't at least try
to make the team, she would never realize her ambition**.
It's a good thing she didn't let fear or uncertainty keep
her from trying out. She did brilliantly and made the
team, then won a silver medal for her country.

The Pen Is Mightier Than the Sword

(the written word is more powerful than physical force)

It's true! **The pen is mightier than the sword!** I just got a letter from the president of the corporation that made my car. I've been having trouble with the alignment and the steering column almost from the day I bought it.

Did you take it back to the dealer?

I sure did, but he kept claiming that everything seemed OK. I got so angry that I almost came to blows with the guy, but I decided against force and instead I wrote a letter to the president of the company. As you can see, he wrote back and not only did he apologize for the way I was treated, he offered to let me trade in the car for a brand new one at no additional cost!

Congratulations! You've proved that **the written word is more powerful than physical force**.

Practice Makes Perfect

(doing something many times improves one's skill at it)

You're now typing thirty words per minute. Good for you. That's a big improvement.

Thank you. If only I could stop making mistakes on those numbers!

That's something you'll have to work on, but **practice makes perfect**. Eventually you'll be able to type the numbers just as accurately as you do the letters.

Now that you mention it, I have been concentrating more on the letters. I think I'll focus my practice on the numbers for a while. **With constant drill and repetition I should be able to type them perfectly.**

You'll increase your typing speed and proficiency, too. Just keep practicing. You can only get better!

Rome Wasn't Built in a Day

(important things do not happen overnight)

Hi, Judy. How's your word processing class coming along?

Well, so far progress has been rather slow. I haven't learned the keyboard yet, and I have problems remembering all the commands for editing. I get really impatient because I want to master the technique as soon as possible.

Just remember that **Rome wasn't built in a day**. Word processing can be a complicated procedure.

You're right. Our teacher keeps telling us that it takes time to learn all the aspects of word processing and that **we can't master everything in one day**.

That's absolutely true. But you'll catch on. Just be patient and practice whenever you can.

The Squeaking Wheel Gets the Oil

(those who complain the loudest get the most attention)

Hi, Ian. What have you been up to?

Not much. Actually, I've been thinking of moving.

Why's that?

My apartment is a mess. The paint is chipping. There's a leak in the ceiling and the linoleum in the kitchen is cracked. What annoys me the most is that all the other apartments in the building have been completely renovated, except mine.

For heaven's sake! Haven't you learned that **the squeaking wheel gets the oil**?

Well, I've mentioned the problems to the building manager, but so far nothing has been done.

Maybe you haven't stated your complaints forcefully enough. Remember, **those who complain the loudest get the most attention**.

You're Never Too Old to Learn

(a person can learn at any age)

Chinese! What are you doing studying Chinese?

I've always wanted to learn it, but I never got around to it before. All those years I was so involved with business that there was never any time. Now that I'm retired, I thought I'd give it a shot. I figure **you're never too old to learn**.

More power to you. I've been thinking of going back to school myself, but I'm getting up in years and I didn't know if I was too old to learn.

Listen, my friend. **A person can learn at any age.** You can do it if you want to badly enough. Just stick with it.

I appreciate your words of encouragement. Maybe I will take that class in real estate, after all.

Section Five

It Never Works

Beggars Can't Be Choosers

(when a person has nothing, he or she must accept whatever help is offered)

What's up, Jennifer? I heard you were in a little accident the other day.

Yeah. This guy bumped into the back of my car when I stopped at an intersection.

Was there much damage to your car?

Well, enough that I had to leave it at a body shop for several days.

How did you get around?

The shop gave me a "loaner," but it ran very poorly.

For heaven's sake! Why did you accept it?

Beggars can't be choosers. I needed another car until mine was repaired, so **I had to accept whatever the shop offered me**.

Clothes Do Not Make the Man

(a person should not be judged by the clothes he or she wears)

I saw Howard the other day in a costume store. He was renting a suit of armor for a costume ball. Sally's going to be there, and he thinks she might agree to go out with him if he projects a more manly image.

He must be dreaming! Doesn't he know that **clothes do not make the man**?

He's convinced that Sally has always refused his invitations because of his puny appearance. Evidently he doesn't realize that **she's not going to judge his character by observing the clothes he's wearing**.

You said it! A suit of armor won't change his appearance or his personality. Still, I wish him luck.

A Leopard Cannot Change His Spots

(a person cannot change his or her basic character once it has been formed)

Pat, I'm at my wits' end. I don't know what to do about having Stephen clean up his room.

Didn't he promise to tidy it up this afternoon?

He did. And look at it. It's still a mess! I can't and won't keep picking up after him.

It looks like **a leopard cannot change his spots**. No matter what we do, he won't keep his room in order.

Please don't expect me to believe that **his habits are already formed and he can't change them**. He's too young for that.

OK. I'll have a talk with him and see what I can do.

Good luck. But I bet you won't get to first base with him.

Man Does Not Live by Bread Alone

(people's psychological needs as well as their physical needs must be satisfied if they are to live)

Holy cow, Pete! Don't you think about anything but food? After all, **man does not live by bread alone**.

Look! Don't go around thinking that all I care about is food. I know that **there's more to life than eating**. After all, who but me is doing twenty hours a week of volunteer work at the community center? And who do you suppose spends his weekends as a big brother for underprivileged children?

I've never doubted your dedication to helping others. I just think your dedication to food might be somewhat exaggerated. All that extra weight you're carrying around isn't doing your heart any good.

Money Does Not Grow on Trees

(money is not easily obtained)

I can't wait to show you the fabric I found for the drapes in the living room and dining room. I saw the perfect carpeting for the family room, too. Now we just need to pick out some furniture.

Hold it! We just paid a hefty sum of money for the down payment on the house. The landscaping also cost a bundle. We'll have to take it easy for a while. After all, **money does not grow on trees.**

I know that **money is not easy to come by,** but where will we sit if we have no furniture?

What's wrong with our old furniture?

It won't match the new carpeting and drapes!

Then we'll just have to sit on the floor.

One Swallow Does Not a Summer Make

(one piece of evidence is not enough to prove something)

Hey, Rebecca. How was your tennis match the other day?

Great! I beat out García and made the final play-offs. I've got the championship in the bag!

Hold on, there. I can understand your excitement, but remember that **one swallow does not a summer make.** The final outcome won't be known until the last game is played.

You're right. I know I shouldn't **form my opinion based on a single victory,** but I've got a good feeling about this tournament.

More power to you. I hope you don't end up by being disappointed.

Too Many Chiefs,
Not Enough Indians

**(too many people are giving orders, and not
enough people are following orders)**

What's going on here? I told you guys to get these
trucks loaded and have them ready to roll out two hours
ago! Why is the job only half done?

Well, boss, the trouble is that you weren't around, and
**everybody had his own idea on how the job should be
done. Since nobody would listen to anyone else, we
couldn't do the job.**

Oh, I see. **Too many chiefs, not enough Indians.**

You've got it!

OK. Let's get it together. From now on I'll be giving the
orders and you guys will be following through. If
everybody keeps trying to run the show, nothing will ever
get done.

You Can Lead a Horse to Water, but You Can't Make Him Drink

(you can propose a course of action to someone, but you can't force that person to accept it)

Did you enjoy your dinner at that new French restaurant last night?

I sure did, but Larry might as well not have come. I ordered the house special and both the waiter and I recommended that Larry do the same, but he ended up ordering what he could have had in any coffee shop—a cheeseburger and fries! Imagine that!

Well, you know what they say: **you can lead a horse to water, but you can't make him drink.** If I remember correctly, Larry has always stuck to American cuisine.

That's true. And I realize that **you can suggest to another person what he should do, but you can't make him take your advice.** I guess I'll just have to keep Larry away from continental cuisine until he's ready to try something new.

You Can't Have Your Cake and Eat It Too

(you can't enjoy the advantages of two conflicting activities at once)

Are we going to see you at Bill's place tonight?

I don't think I'll be able to make it. I've been getting a little static from my wife about our weekly "boy's night out." She's getting tired of being left alone every Friday night. We had a bit of a tiff, and she came right out and told me: **"You can't have your cake and eat it too!"**

Gee, that's too bad. You'll be missed.

And I'll miss seeing you guys. But she's right. Now that I'm married **I can't keep enjoying the advantages of bachelorhood without jeopardizing my relationship with my wife.**

I understand, and I'll let the other guys know. But don't hesitate to drop in any time you happen to be free in the future. You'll always be welcome.

You Can't Teach an Old Dog New Tricks

(elderly people can't change their behavior or learn anything new)

To many of his friends, Mr. Jones seemed quite eccentric. Although he was getting on in years, he had a long-standing habit of going out alone to walk in a shoddy part of town late at night. His friends warned him that this was a dangerous practice, and they advised him to do his walking during the day. However, he made no effort to change his routine. It was evident that **you can't teach an old dog new tricks.** Even his closest friends had to accept the fact that **it's almost impossible for an elderly person to adopt a new routine.**

Section Six

It's Human Nature

The Apple Doesn't Fall Far from the Tree

(children take after their parents)

Well, Mr. West, this rash is nothing serious. Just apply this ointment, and it should be gone in a few days.

Thanks, doctor. By the way, how is your son doing?

Great! He's in his second year of medical school, and doing quite well.

Ah! **The apple doesn't fall far from the tree.**

So it seems. Actually, I'm very proud of him. He says that he wants to specialize in heart surgery.

That's ambitious. I'm sure you're pleased that **your son is following in your footsteps by going into medicine.**

Yes, that makes me happy. He should make a fine surgeon.

Barking Dogs Seldom Bite

(people who threaten others usually do not hurt them)

Hi, Frank. What are you doing back in class today? I thought Mr. Tucker kicked you out yesterday for misbehaving.

He did. But you know that **barking dogs seldom bite.** I've had Mr. Tucker for other classes, so I know that he never stays angry for long. **He has threatened to punish other students before, but he has seldom followed through.** Actually, he's a very forgiving person.

So how did you get him to let you back in?

I went to his office after class and apologized for causing such a ruckus. I gave him my word that it would never happen again. Sure enough, he accepted my apology, and here I am!

Better a Live Coward Than a Dead Hero

(it's better to run from a life-threatening situation than to fight and risk being killed)

Mathieu had made a career of the army, and over the years he had seen battle numerous times. He had never distinguished himself in any particular way, but he had managed to come out alive from some truly life-threatening situations. His basic philosophy had always been: **better a live coward than a dead hero.** Frankly, that's how he managed to stay alive. He was no hero, and he didn't want to be. **He preferred to run from danger rather than die in an act of bravery.**

A Fool and His Money Are Soon Parted

(a foolish person quickly spends his or her money on worthless things)

Rick had always thrown caution to the winds when it came to money. He would often spend his money carelessly on things he really didn't need. When he won a large sum of money in the lottery, he was very excited. However, **a fool and his money are soon parted.** First Rick went on a shopping spree, and then he invited some friends to spend the weekend at a fancy, expensive resort. It was not long before he went through every cent he had won. **He foolishly spent his winnings on worthless and unnecessary things,** and soon he had nothing left. How easy it would have been to put some of the money away for a rainy day.

He Who Laughs Last, Laughs Best

(the person who succeeds in making the last move has the most fun)

I still can't believe it! Sue Carlson, the homecoming queen, was Caleb's date at the prom last night.

That *is* one for the books! She's one of the most beautiful girls in school. I thought for sure she would be going with Al, the captain of the football team. Caleb is such a bookworm. What does she see in him?

Evidently Al was taking Sue for granted and assumed she would go to the prom with him without his even asking her. Caleb wooed her with compliments and a book of love poems, so she agreed to go with him. When Al found out, he hit the ceiling!

It just goes to show you that **he who laughs last, laughs best.**

Who would have ever believed it? Al has always been so cocky.

Yes, but **Caleb really came out on top in this situation and won the lasting victory.**

Old Habits Die Hard

(it is very difficult to change an established pattern of behavior)

When I ran into Neil the other day he was coughing up a storm. Is he OK?

Who knows? He's as OK as he'll ever be.

I don't get you.

He's taken up smoking again. You know he had quit for about a year, but I guess **old habits die hard.** The doctor even warned him that he would have health problems if he continued to smoke.

What made him start again?

As I said, **it's very difficult to change a set habit.** He was doing quite well until he had some personal problems. He must have started smoking again to alleviate the strain of dealing with them.

That's too bad. His health is bound to suffer.

One Man's Gravy Is Another Man's Poison

(what is pleasing to one person may not be pleasing to another)

Elaine, we haven't been out for a while. Why don't we take in the symphony tomorrow night?

Charles, you know I've never been able to sit through an entire concert of classical music. How about going to hear that new rock group at Danny's instead?

And get my ears blown off? No way!

It just goes to show you that **one man's gravy is another man's poison.**

Well, I realize that **what pleases one person may not please someone else.** But let's compromise. Come to the symphony concert tomorrow night, and on Saturday I'll take you to hear that rock group. Is it a deal?

OK. I'll even get you a set of ear plugs so you won't go deaf.

The Spirit Is Willing, but the Flesh Is Weak

(a person's body is not always as strong as his or her mind)

Greetings, Elena. Where have you been keeping yourself lately?

Hi, Paula. Actually, I've been working out at the gym and doing aerobic dance.

It really shows! What prompted you to go in for all this exercise?

I had my yearly checkup, and Dr. Mena told me that I had to lose twenty pounds.

So he put you on a diet, right?

He sure did! But I couldn't stay with it. I would lose five or six pounds, and then I'd put the weight right back on again. The truth is I can't keep away from food.

I see. **The spirit is willing, but the flesh is weak.**

Absolutely right! **I want to lose the weight, but I don't have the willpower to ignore those gnawing pangs of hunger.** Since I love to eat, I decided to exercise in addition to trying to diet. That way I can burn off any extra calories.

You're obviously succeeding. I've never seen you look better.

There Is No Honor among Thieves

(one dishonest person cannot trust another)

After the bank robbery, the members of the gang decided to split up and go in different directions in order to avoid getting picked up by the police. The leader of the gang said that he would hold all the money and distribute it to the other members after pressure from the authorities had died down. All the robbers agreed and went their separate ways. Needless to say, none of them ever received his share of the money. They should have known better, for **there is no honor among thieves.** In time, all the gang members were caught and sentenced to long prison terms. There they remained, fully aware of the fact that **one dishonest person cannot trust another.**

There's More Than One Way to Skin a Cat

(there are many ways to achieve a goal)

Meinhard, what answer did you get for that equation? I came out with forty-five.

So did I! Could I see how you arrived at your answer? Sure. Be my guest.

Let's take a look. I used different calculations in steps two and three.

It doesn't matter. We both got the same answer, didn't we?

We sure did!

See. **There's more than one way to skin a cat.**

That's what counts. It just goes to show you that **the same goal can be achieved in more than one way.** Math certainly is no exception.

There's No Fool like an Old Fool

(a foolish act seems even more foolish when performed by an older person, who should have a lot of wisdom)

Did you hear about Henry? He's gotten married again.

I can't believe it! At his age? This is his third time, isn't it?

Yeah. **There's no fool like an old fool.** You'd think he would have learned when his first two marriages ended in disaster. I honestly don't see how this one can last, either.

What makes you think that?

Henry's job. It requires long hours and keeps him away from home six months out of the year.

It seems that ol' Henry hasn't learned anything from his previous relationships. He's already got two strikes against him—his age and his job. And **there's nothing more ridiculous than the foolish behavior of a person who should have learned something from his previous experiences.**

Variety Is the Spice of Life

(differences and changes make life enjoyable)

How was your trip to New York?

We had a marvelous time! New York really has a lot to offer. We took in a couple of Broadway shows, had dinner at some fancy restaurants, met all kinds of interesting people, shopped on Fifth Avenue, and visited the Metropolitan Museum of Art.

Sounds great! You saw and did a great deal on your vacation. It must have been quite enjoyable.

It sure was! It's true that **variety is the spice of life!** We hadn't had a vacation for a long time, so **we took great pleasure in doing many different things to make our stay as enjoyable as possible.** We'll remember this vacation for a long time.

When the Cat's Away the Mice Will Play

(some people will misbehave when they are not being watched)

Orlando, are you going on that Alaskan cruise with your parents?

No, Mrs. Stevenson. I've got to stick around for school.

Then you'll have the house all to yourself.

That's right. My folks'll be gone for ten days. I was thinking of having a party this weekend to celebrate Susanna's birthday.

Oh, I see. **When the cat's away the mice will play.**

Not exactly. Mom might have said OK. She likes Susanna. Anyway, **since my folks won't be around to say no, I see no reason for us not to have a little fun.**

It looks like your mind is made up. You want to have the party, even if it might go against your parents' wishes.

Don't worry. We'll be extra careful, and I'll tell Mom and Dad about the party as soon as they get back.

Section Seven

Friend or Foe?

Absence Makes the Heart Grow Fonder

(people often feel more affectionate toward each other when they are apart)

Say, Peter. I haven't seen you with Lillian these days. Where has she been hiding out?

She's been traveling overseas for the past two months. To tell you the truth, I never thought I'd miss her so much.

They say that **absence makes the heart grow fonder.**

It's true in my case, anyway. I guess I was taking Lillian for granted. I didn't realize how much she means to me until she was gone.

I think most people react the same way. **When two people are separated, they often feel more affectionate toward each other.** Tell me. When is Lillian due back?

In a couple of weeks. I can hardly wait.

Beauty Is in the Eye
of the Beholder

(what seems ordinary or ugly to one person might seem beautiful to another)

I still can't figure out how Janet could have fallen for Paul. He's no prize at all!

When you come right down to it, she's nothing to rave about either. Clearly, **beauty is in the eye of the beholder.**

I'll second that! **What appears attractive to one person might seem ugly or ordinary to someone else.** I guess we should remember that looks aren't everything.

You're right. Janet and Paul are both very nice people.

Blood Is Thicker Than Water

(members of the same family share stronger ties with each other than they do with others)

Hi, Gina. I'm here to pick up your truck. Remember? You promised to let me borrow it for the day.

That I did, but I'm going to have to disappoint you. My brother took the truck this morning to pick up some furniture at a warehouse. He needed it right away, so I gave it to him.

Boy, that really leaves me high and dry, but I guess **blood is thicker than water.**

Don't take it personally. This was a very pressing matter. Besides, he should be back in a couple of hours. Then the truck's yours. By the way, I gave my brother the truck because he needed it right away, not because **family members share stronger ties with each other than they do with others.** I would have done the same for you if you had been in his position.

Familiarity Breeds Contempt

**(when you know people well you will
discover their weaknesses and you may
come to scorn them)**

Ms. Carruthers was appointed head librarian because of
her organizational abilities and her plans for improving
the library's services. At first, the other staff members
appreciated her ideas and enthusiasm. But after several
weeks of working with her, they began to resent her
frequent memos and meetings. The more they learned
about her management style, the less they liked it. As one
librarian said to another, **Familiarity breeds contempt.**
The library staff welcomed Ms. Carruthers and her ideas
at first, but **after they got to know her better their respect
for her changed to dislike and scorn.**

A Friend in Need Is a Friend Indeed

(a true friend will help you in a time of trouble)

Serge, I hear you're having some trouble with American lit. I've already taken that course. Maybe I can help you out.

No kidding? Do you have the time?

Sure. My time is your time.

A friend in need is a friend indeed!

Come on, I wouldn't let you down! We've been pals for a long time, and I know you'd help me out if I needed it. After all, **true friends come to your aid whenever you need them.**

I'm glad you feel that way. I do, too. Now, I'd like to get your interpretation of this passage from *Tom Sawyer*.

No problem. I remember when we discussed it in class.

A Friend Who Shares Is a Friend Who Cares

**(a true friend unselfishly shares
what he or she has)**

Hi, Janet. What brings you to Benito's Pizza Parlor today?

Oh. Hi, Jud. I'm treating myself to a nice lunch. You know, this place serves the best pizza around. Have a seat and join me. I've got more than enough for the both of us.

If you insist! I suppose I could take that small piece there off your hands.

Be my guest! After all, **a friend who shares is a friend who cares.**

Thanks. The feeling's mutual. **True friends show that they really care about you by unselfishly sharing what they have.**

Don't give it a second thought. I know you would do the same for me.

Imitation Is the Sincerest Form of Flattery

(trying to be like someone is the most genuine way of praising that person)

Well, Cindy. What do you want to be when you grow up?

I want to be a baseball player, just like Ron Fox. He's my hero. Look at the number of home runs he has hit, and look at how the fans cheer when he comes out on the field.

He certainly is popular and well liked. I can understand why you would want to be like him. After all, **imitation is the sincerest form of flattery.**

I'd give anything to meet him in person and get his autograph.

Perhaps that can be arranged. The team is playing here this Saturday. Maybe we can talk to him and get his autograph after the game. **If you tell him that you want to be a baseball player just like him, he will feel very complimented.**

Gee, Uncle Joe. That would be great! Let's go!

Love Is Blind

(one sees no faults in the person one loves)

I just don't know how Carolyn has stuck it out with Matt for so many years.

They've been married for over thirty years, haven't they?

True—in spite of the fact that he's such a rude and selfish person.

He has been far from the ideal husband, and yet she puts up with him and completely ignores his shortcomings.

No doubt about it, **love is blind!**

You're right. Apparently **she loves him so much that she doesn't see his faults.**

Well, I can't say the same about my husband. I'm not blind to his faults, and he's not blind to mine! But I think we have a good marriage anyway.

Section Eight

Words to Live By

Actions Speak Louder Than Words

(people's actions are more convincing than their words are)

Listen, José. If you intend to ask Consuelo to marry you, you've got to get moving! Why haven't you asked her yet?

I guess I'm afraid to take the plunge, although I know she loves me and I certainly love her.

Well, the other day Mario told me he was going to buy a ring and ask Consuelo to become engaged. You can't just keep talking about marrying Consuelo. You've got to do something about it. Remember: **actions speak louder than words.**

Wow! You're right. **If I want Consuelo to take me seriously, I've got to stop talking about getting engaged and go ask her to marry me.** I just hope I'm not too late.

I don't think you've got anything to worry about. Consuelo has never been that fond of Mario. But if I were you, I'd move quickly. After all, you don't want to take any chances.

Better Late Than Never

(it's better to do something late than not to do it at all)

Finally you're here! We thought you'd never make it. Is everything all right?

Sure, we're fine. Please accept our deepest apologies for arriving so late. We got a flat tire on the freeway, and it took us a while to put on the spare. Anyway, here we are. We hope we haven't inconvenienced you.

Don't give it a second thought. **Better late than never.**

Thanks for being so understanding. We almost called you to cancel our plans after we got the tire changed, but we decided **it would be better to show up late than to not show up at all.**

You did the right thing. We would have been terribly disappointed if you hadn't come. Let's go on to the dining room and eat now.

Better Safe Than Sorry

(it is better to choose a safe course of action than a risky one that could lead to regrets)

Memorial Day weekend is coming up. Why don't we go visit Herb and Stephie in L.A.?

Sure. I'm game. Should we drive or take the train?

I think it'll be faster if we drive. We can be there in six hours.

The way you drive, probably less! But I'd rather not be on the road with all that traffic on Memorial Day weekend. Let's take the train. **Better safe than sorry.**

You're right. A holiday weekend is a dangerous time to take a car trip. **We should take the train and be safe, rather than risk being hurt in a car accident**.

I'm glad you agree. The train it is!

A Bird in the Hand Is Worth Two in the Bush

(something you already have is better than something you might get)

How's your new job coming along, Sasha?

Oh, the job's fine. I have good working hours and the surroundings are very pleasant. There's only one hitch.

What's that?

The salary isn't too great.

That's a shame. Did you interview for any other jobs?

Yes. A couple of them would have paid much better, but I never got an offer from them, so I figured that...

A bird in the hand is worth two in the bush! Right?

Exactly! **I accepted this job rather than waiting for a better offer that might not have come.**

Charity Begins at Home

(one should take care of one's own family, friends, or fellow citizens before helping other people)

You're home late again. What have you been up to?

I've been playing Santa Claus. Last night I was at the children's ward of the hospital, and tonight I stopped off at the orphanage to help wrap gifts and put up the Christmas tree.

That's very nice of you, but **charity begins at home.** Your own children haven't seen you at all lately. Don't you think you should pay some attention to them, too?

You have a point, but we have so much and others have so little. I was just trying to spread some Christmas cheer.

I'm sure your efforts are immensely appreciated, but we need your attention, too. I don't think it's unreasonable to ask you to **take care of your own family before going out to help others.**

Haste Makes Waste

(when one hurries too much, one is likely to do a poor job and have to waste time doing it over)

Jacques, I warned you not to be in such a hurry to clear those dirty dishes off the tables! Now look what you did!

OK. So I slipped and dropped all the plates. Don't get so upset. I'll clean up the mess.

That's not the point. How many times do I have to tell you that **haste makes waste?**

I'll admit that **hurrying often creates problems that must be solved,** but this really wasn't my fault. The floor was slippery.

That's no excuse. If you hadn't been rushing around, you would have been more careful and probably wouldn't have slipped.

Love Makes the World Go Round

(when people show respect and consideration for one another, the world is a better place)

What's wrong, Kumi? Why are you so upset?

It's those new neighbors of ours. They play their stereo so loud at night that I can't sleep. I've had it. I'm going to go over there and give them a piece of my mind!

Hold it! You won't accomplish anything by hollering at them. You're all worked up now. Why not wait until you cool down a bit? Don't you know that **love makes the world go round?**

I agree that **the world would be a better place to live if people respected and loved each other**, but right now . . .

Not another word! Let's try it my way. I'll bake some cookies, and later on we'll take them next door and introduce ourselves. We can casually mention the problem after we get to know our new neighbors. I'm sure they'll cooperate.

One Good Turn
Deserves Another

(a favor should be repaid with another favor)

Eva felt very sorry for her next-door neighbor, Elaine. The two women had been living next to each other for years and had become close friends. Years ago, when Eva lost her husband, Elaine was there to console her and bolster her spirits. Eva had never forgotten the emotional support of her friend, and she strongly believed that **one good turn deserves another**. Now Elaine was quite ill, so Eva made a point of spending the days with her friend, tending to her needs and helping to nurse her back to health. It was not just because she felt that **Elaine's kindness should be repaid with another favor**. Eva was genuinely concerned about her friend and wanted to help her out.

You Have to Take the Good with the Bad

(you must accept disappointment along with success)

Say, John. You look rather depressed. What's up?

That deal I was working on fell through, and the whole matter has gotten me down.

But you should know that in life **you have to take the good with the bad**. Look at it this way. Your last two business transactions worked out quite well, didn't they?

True enough. I guess I'm spoiled.

Come on, don't be so hard on yourself. It's not easy learning that **you must accept disappointments and defeats as well as successes**.

You're right. I'm sure I'll feel better after I have a bite to eat. Come on, let's go out for a hamburger.

You're on!

You Reap What You Sow

**(the amount of effort you put into something
determines how much you will get out of it)**

Chuck felt bad about not going with his friends for pizza
after the school dance, but with a final exam coming up
in a couple of days, he knew that **you reap what you sow**.
As it turned out, his decision to go home and study for
the exam was a good one. **His efforts at studying paid off
with a high grade on the exam.** Unfortunately, his friends
did not score half as well.

Section Nine

Some Things Never Change

After the Feast Comes the Reckoning

(people must always pay the price of their excesses)

Hey, Bill. Is that another new jacket you're wearing?

Yeah. Just got it the other day. Like it?

I sure do. But tell me—lately you've been spending like a madman. Where's all this money coming from?

No problem. I've been buying everything on credit.

Easy there, pal. Aren't you getting in over your head? Remember: **after the feast comes the reckoning**.

I know I've been spending a lot, but so far I've been able to make my monthly payments.

Sure. But what happens if you get laid off? That construction job you have won't last forever, and **you'll still have to pay for your excesses**.

I know, but I'll cross that bridge when and if I get to it.

Bad News Travels Fast

**(reports of problems and misfortune
spread quickly)**

I just heard about Joey's loss. He must have taken it
quite hard.

He sure did! His investments were completely wiped
out when the price of those speculative stocks fell. But
how did you find out so soon?

Bad news travels fast! The office staff has been talking
about nothing else. People say he's pretty broken up.

No doubt about it! It's amazing the way **news about
people's problems spreads so quickly**.

Well, knowing Joey I'm sure he'll get back on his feet
in no time. He has a knack for making money. He won't
let this bad break keep him down.

The Best Things in Life Are Free

(the things that give a person the most happiness don't cost anything)

Good afternoon, Mrs. Thompson. It's nice seeing you again. How did you enjoy the holidays?

They were really special for me. We had a big family reunion with all my children and grandchildren. I can't tell you the joy that their visit brought to our home.

I can certainly understand how you must have felt to have your family around you. After all, **the best things in life are free.**

Absolutely! We spent many happy hours doing things as a family and playing with the grandchildren. Just think! **Those hours that gave us such satisfaction and joy didn't cost a penny!**

How wonderful! It sure would be hard to top that!

The Bigger They Are, the Harder They Fall

(the more important someone is, the more severe are the consequences of his or her failure)

Say, Ramon. I heard that Phil Jacobson is moving out to the West Coast. What's going on?

I heard that he was dismissed from that big corporation he directed for the past fifteen years.

Boy! That's quite a blow!

It sure is. **The bigger they are, the harder they fall!** Rumor has it that he led the corporation into insolvency by approving high-risk loans and bad investments.

I guess he deserved what he got.

Even so, I feel kind of sorry for the guy. **The more important you are, the worse it must be to fail.**

Phil's a tough young man, though. He'll get back on his feet soon.

Good Things Come in Small Packages

(small containers can hold objects of great value)

I was truly surprised on my birthday. I didn't expect such a lovely gift.

Your gold bracelet is gorgeous! Did you get many other gifts?

Yes, and most of them came in big boxes with fancy wrapping paper. Of course, I couldn't resist opening them first. I got some sweaters and shoes that I wanted, but the bracelet came in the smallest box—which I opened last.

There you go. **Good things come in small packages.**

How true. Not only did I get the bracelet, but I got two small charms to put on it as well. **Wonderful objects can indeed be found in small containers.** This has been the best birthday ever for me!

I hope you have many more just as nice as this one!

The Grass Is Always Greener on the Other Side of the Fence

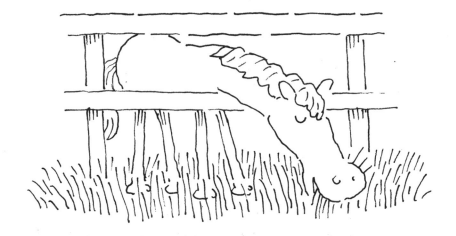

(another place or situation always appears to be better than your own)

Jim and Alex had been friends since childhood, but as adults their lives went in different directions. Jim achieved great success in business, while Alex worked as a clerk in a department store. Although Alex was basically happy with his job, he would often think that **the grass is always greener on the other side of the fence** when he considered Jim's financial success. It appeared to Alex that **his friend was much better off and in a more advantageous position than he was**. What Alex did not know was that Jim was not happy with his job and that his health was suffering because of the constant stress.

Hindsight Is Better Than Foresight

(people see and understand things more clearly after they've happened than before they've happened)

Say, Boris. How's the import-export business these days?

Generally, booming. But I'm losing out on a lot of business with Japanese firms because of my inability to communicate in Japanese. I really regret not studying the language years ago, when I had the chance.

Unfortunately, **hindsight is better than foresight**.

True enough, but **now that I realize what I should have done, I'm sorry that I didn't have the foresight to do it before.**

Oh, well. It's never too late to learn. Why not check out the language program at City College? They usually offer classes in Japanese.

I just might do that. Thanks for the info.

It Never Rains but It Pours

(good and bad things tend to happen in groups)

Whew! I've had it! Thank heavens they're finally gone. If they had stayed one more day, I would have gone out of my mind.

I'll admit our guests overstayed their welcome, but don't worry. We'll rest up this weekend.

Have you forgotten that your folks are scheduled to arrive tomorrow?

Holy smokes! **It never rains but it pours!** And they said they wanted to stay through the holidays.

Why is it that **troublesome situations never come up one at a time? They always seem to happen all at once**.

I'll call Mom and Dad and ask them if they can put off their visit for a week. I'm sure they'll understand. We need some time by ourselves.

Lightning Never Strikes Twice in the Same Place

(the same misfortune won't happen twice to the same person)

Hi, Gus. I'm glad to see you're up and about.

Thanks. After that truck plowed into my car last month, I thought it was all over for me. I'm really lucky to be alive.

That's for sure. It must have been quite a traumatic experience for you. Has your car been repaired yet?

Yes, it has. But I won't be driving it anymore. I'm not taking any chances on being hit again.

Come on, now. You can't let one unfortunate incident keep you from ever driving again. **Lightning never strikes twice in the same place.**

That's what people say, but it's hard for me to believe that **a person can't encounter the same type of misfortune twice.** For the time being, I'll be taking public transportation to work.

Might Makes Right

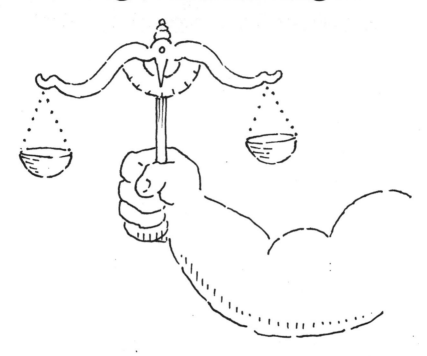

(the stronger of two opponents will always control the situation)

Hi, Maya. I see you're studying for the history exam tomorrow.

I'm trying, but I get so distressed reading about all the people and countries that have been taken over by superior armed forces. Why is it so hard for people to live and let live?

Haven't you heard? **Might makes right!** All through the course of history **the stronger of two opponents has always won out over the weaker one**.

Sure. I guess it's human nature, but that doesn't excuse all the violence that takes place when one nation subdues another one.

Don't let it get you down now. You need to go into that exam with a clear head. What was, was. What will be, will be.

No News Is Good News

(if one does not hear the outcome of a situation, that outcome must be positive)

Hello, Luís. Where have you been keeping yourself lately?

Oh, I've been busy fixing up the condo.

No wonder I haven't seen you around. By the way, what do you hear from your roommate?

Not a word for a month now. **I guess no news is good news.**

It's too bad he had to leave so suddenly. What was the problem?

There was a serious illness in his family. I asked him to keep me informed, but **since I've received no information, everything must be OK so far**.

I sure hope so. I know you'll be glad when he gets back.

Nothing Hurts like the Truth

(it is painful to discover an unpleasant truth about oneself)

Since childhood Jan had a flair for music, and as he was growing up he trained long and hard for a career as a concert pianist. Although he believed he played well, in truth he was not particularly gifted. He refused to accept this fact, and against his teacher's wishes he decided to give a debut recital. The critics all praised his performance; nevertheless, they were unanimous in their opinion that he did not have the necessary talent to become a great concert artist. Upon reading the reviews, Jan thought that **nothing hurts like the truth**. For the first time he became aware of his shortcomings, and **it pained him greatly to accept the fact that he lacked the talent to play on the concert stage.**

Possession Is Nine-Tenths of the Law

(the person who possesses something has the strongest claim to owning it)

Say, Chris, that's a nice gold chain you're wearing. Did you buy it, or did someone give it to you?

Why are you asking?

Well, it looks just like the one I lost a couple of days ago.

To tell you the truth, I found it on the sidewalk on my way home from school. And what's more, I intend to keep it! After all, **possession is nine-tenths of the law**.

Yeah, but it doesn't really belong to you. What if it's mine?

How are you going to prove it? Your chain wasn't one of a kind. **Since this chain is in my possession now, I lay claim to it.** Maybe you misplaced yours somewhere. Why not look around? It could very well turn up.

The Proof of the Pudding Is in the Eating

(the only way to judge something is to try it)

Hey, Pete. How come you don't go out for the basketball team?

Oh, I don't know, coach. I've never had any interest in sports.

But you'd be a natural! I've been observing you in gym class. You're fast and well coordinated, and you have good height.

Yeah, but basketball isn't my thing.

At least you could give it a try. What do you have to lose? **The proof of the pudding is in the eating.**

I never really thought about it. Maybe it would be fun.

Now you're talking! **Give it a try so you can find out if you really like it or not.**

OK, coach. You talked me into it. I'll try out for the team if you agree to let me bow out if I decide I don't like it.

Index of Proverbs

Don't count your chickens before they're hatched (don't plan on the successful results of something until those results actually occur) 24

Don't cry over spilt milk (don't grieve about having done something that cannot be undone) 25

Don't judge a book by its cover (don't form an opinion about something based on appearance alone) 26

Don't judge a man until you've walked in his boots (don't criticize a person until you've tried to do the things he does) 27

Don't look a gift horse in the mouth (don't complain about something that is given to you) 28

Don't put all your eggs in one basket (don't risk losing everything at once) 29

Don't put off for tomorrow what you can do today (don't unnecessarily postpone doing something) 30

Don't put the cart before the horse (don't do things in the wrong order) 31

F

Familiarity breeds contempt (when you know people well you will discover their weaknesses and you may come to scorn them) 73

The first step is always the hardest (the most difficult part of accomplishing something is getting started) 35

A fool and his money are soon parted (a foolish person quickly spends his or her money on worthless things) 60

Forewarned is forearmed (being warned about something before it happens allows a person to prepare for it) 36

A friend in need is a friend indeed (a true friend will help you in a time of trouble) 74

A friend who shares is a friend who cares (a true friend unselfishly shares what he or she has) 75

G

Good things come in small packages (small containers can hold objects of great value) 92

The grass is always greener on the other side of the fence (another place or situation always appears to be better than your own) 93

H

Haste makes waste (when one hurries too much, one is likely to do a poor job and have to waste time doing it over) 83

He who hesitates is lost (a person who doesn't act decisively is unlikely to succeed) 37

He who laughs last, laughs best (the person who succeeds in making the last move has the most fun) 61

Hindsight is better than foresight (people see and understand things more clearly after they've happened than before they've happened) 94

I

If at first you don't succeed, try, try again (persevere until you reach your goal) 38

If you can't beat them, join them (if you can't defeat your opponents, join forces with them) 12

If you can't stand the heat, get out of the kitchen (if you can't tolerate the pressures of a particular situation, remove yourself from that situation) 13

Imitation is the sincerest form of flattery (trying to be like someone is the most genuine way of praising that person) 76

In unity there is strength (a group of people with the same goals can accomplish more than individuals can) 2

It never rains but it pours (good
and bad things tend to happen
in groups)   95

It takes two to tango (when two
people work as a team, they
are both responsible for the
team's successes and
failures)   3

L

Leave well enough alone (don't try
to improve something that is
already satisfactory)   14

A leopard cannot change his spots
(a person cannot change his or
her basic character once it has
been formed)   49

**Lightning never strikes twice in
the same place** (the same
misfortune won't happen
twice to the same person)   96

Look before you leap (consider all
aspects of a situation before
you take any action)   15

Love is blind (one sees no faults in
the person one loves)   77

Love makes the world go round
(when people show respect
and consideration for one
another, the world is a better
place)   84

M

Make hay while the sun shines
(take advantage of an
opportunity to do
something)   16

Man does not live by bread alone
(people's psychological needs
as well as their physical needs
must be satisfied if they are to
live)   50

**A man is known by the company
he keeps** (a person is believed
to be like the people with
whom he or she spends
time)   4

Might makes right (the stronger of
two opponents will always
control the situation)   97

Misery loves company (unhappy
people often get satisfaction
from having others share their
misery)   5

A miss is as good as a mile (losing
by a narrow margin is no

different than losing by a wide
margin)   32

Money does not grow on trees
(money is not easily
obtained)   51

N

**Necessity is the mother of
invention** (most inventions are
created to solve a
problem)   39

No news is good news (if one does
not hear the outcome of a
situation, that outcome must
be positive)   98

No pain, no gain (nothing can be
accomplished without
effort)   40

Nothing hurts like the truth (it is
painful to discover an
unpleasant truth about
oneself)   99

Nothing ventured, nothing gained
(you can't achieve anything if
you don't try)   41

O

Old habits die hard (it is very
difficult to change an
established pattern of
behavior)   62

One good turn deserves another (a
favor should be repaid with
another favor)   85

**One man's gravy is another man's
poison** (what is pleasing to one
person may not be pleasing to
another)   63

**One swallow does not a summer
make** (one piece of evidence is
not enough to prove
something)   52

P

**The pen is mightier than the
sword** (the written word is
more powerful than physical
force)   42

**Possession is nine-tenths of the
law** (the person who possesses
something has the strongest
claim to owning it)   100

Practice makes perfect (doing
something many times
improves one's skill at it)   43

The proof of the pudding is in the eating (the only way to judge something is to try it)   101

R

The road to hell is paved with good intentions (good intentions don't always lead to good actions)   33

Rome wasn't built in a day (important things do not · happen overnight)   44

S

The spirit is willing, but the flesh is weak (a person's body is not always as strong as his or her mind)   64

The squeaking wheel gets the oil (those who complain the loudest get the most attention)   45

Strike while the iron is hot (act at the best possible time)   17

T

There is no honor among thieves (one dishonest person cannot trust another)   65

There's more than one way to skin a cat (there are many ways to achieve a goal)   66

There's no fool like an old fool (a foolish act seems even more foolish when performed by an older person, who should have a lot of wisdom)   67

There's no place like home (a person is happiest with his or her family and friends)   6

Too many chiefs, not enough Indians (too many people are giving orders, and not enough people are following orders)   53

Too many cooks spoil the broth (too many people trying to take care of something can ruin it)   7

Two heads are better than one (two people working together can solve a problem quicker and better than a person working alone)   8

Two's company, but three's a crowd (couples often enjoy their privacy and dislike having a third person around)   9

V

Variety is the spice of life (differences and changes make life enjoyable)   68

W

The way to a man's heart is through his stomach (the way to gain a man's love is by preparing food that he enjoys)   18

When in Rome do as the Romans do (when traveling, follow the customs of the local people)   19

When the cat's away the mice will play (some people will misbehave when they are not being watched)   69

Where there's smoke, there's fire (when there is evidence of a problem, there probably is a problem)   34

Y

You can lead a horse to water, but you can't make him drink (you can propose a course of action to someone, but you can't force that person to accept it)   54

You can't have your cake and eat it too (you can't enjoy the advantages of two conflicting activities at once)   55

You can't teach an old dog new tricks (elderly people can't change their behavior or learn anything new)   56

You have to take the good with the bad (you must accept disappointment along with success)   86

You reap what you sow (the amount of effort you put into something determines how much you will get out of it)   87

You're never too old to learn (a person can learn at any age)   41